spill

spill

SCENES OF
BLACK FEMINIST
FUGITIVITY

Alexis Pauline Gumbs

Duke University Press / Durham and London / 2016

© 2016 Duke University Press
Printed in the United States of America on acid-free paper ∞
Designed by Heather Hensley
Typeset in Chaparral Pro by Tseng Information Systems, Inc.

Library of Congress Cataloging-in-Publication Data
Names: Gumbs, Alexis Pauline, [date] author.
Title: Spill : scenes of black feminist fugitivity /
Alexis Pauline Gumbs.
Description: Durham : Duke University Press, 2016. |
Includes bibliographical references and index.
Identifiers: LCCN 2016015534
ISBN 9780822362562 (hardcover : alk. paper)
ISBN 9780822362722 (pbk. : alk. paper)
ISBN 9780822373575 (e-book)
Subjects: LCSH: Spillers, Hortense J. Black,
white and in color—Poetry.
Classification: LCC PS3607.U5459 S65 2016 |
DDC 810.9/89607300904—dc23
LC record available at https://lccn.loc.gov/2016015534

Cover art: Kenyatta A.C. Hinkle, *Now There Are Three Ways to Get
This Done: Your Way, Their Way or My Way*, 2014, India ink, oil pastel,
acrylic paint, and collage, 48 x 36". Created for The Tituba Black
Witch of Salem Drawing Series inspired by "I, Tituba Black Witch
of Salem," by Maryse Condé, 1994. Image courtesy of Kenyatta A.C.
Hinkle and Jenkins Johnson Gallery.

TO BLACK WOMEN
who make and break narrative

/ / /

after and with
Black White and In Color
by Hortense Spillers

CONTENTS

spill

spil/

verb

Origin

*Old English spillan,
"kill, destroy, waste,
shed (blood)";
of unknown origin.*

A NOTE

And so I was trying to ask the question again, ask it anew,

as if it had not been asked before, because the language

of the historian was not telling me what I needed to know.

Which is, what is it like in the interstitial spaces where

you fall between everyone who has a name, a category,

a sponsor, an agenda, spokespersons, people looking out

for them—but you don't have anybody.

—HORTENSE SPILLERS

This writing started to spill out one day when I was listening to Hortense Spillers speak at the Feminist Theory workshop at Duke University. I had been reading and writing about Spillers for years, but something became clear that day about my relationship to her work. What kept me coming back to her essays over and over again was not only what she said (though what she says about race, gender, capitalism, and literature is enough to come back for forever); it was also *how* she said it. Again and again, there were phrases in her work that did far more than make her point. They made worlds. They invited affect. They brought to mind nameless women in unknown places who were laughing and looking sideways at each other and a world that couldn't understand them.

I started this experiment thinking that I could take specific phrases from particular essays in *Black, White, and in Color* out of context, and then I realized that I could never take them out of context. Or that context couldn't take them at all. Which is to say that when I turned these phrases, doors opened and everyone came through. All the black women writers Spillers wrote about and didn't write about. All the characters those black women writers acknowledged and ignored. All the people living novelistic lives without arcs or arks to save them. As usual, the project took over and offered scene after scene out of time and invited voices and settings that I can't claim to have invented. It is either that I was craving these scenes and these voices or they were craving me and we met up at the hot spot called *Black, White, and in Color*.

This space, which is a temporary space, which we must leave, for the sake of future travelers and our own necks, is a sacred dedicated space. Libation for the named and the nameless. This is for black women who made and broke narrative. The quiet, the quarrelling, the queer. This is where. This is what. This is how.

spill (v) 1. cause or allow (liquid) to flow over the edge of its container, especially unintentionally.

"You'll spill that coffee if you're not careful."

SYNONYMS: *knock over, tip over, upset, overturn*

the ground shakes with us
the gathering women
grows rich grows brown grows deep
the gathered hands women
grown brown grown women
the sure determined feet
the ground grows everything we eat
the graceful stomping women heading home
ungrateful women populating poems
the ground has everything it needs
we have never been alone

the sky sings for us
the rainmaking women the rage-taking women
the blood
the sky so open so nose wide open
can't refuse the shape of our lungs
can't bear to remain above
the sky sees the shoulders that shrug off hate
and celebrate and hug
the sky slows the rhythm by falling out
and down and done and drug
the sky begins to know itself
we breathe it in as love

the water waits for us
the wide-eyed women the walking women the worst
the water washes the war wrung women
the wailers the whistle the first

the water waists of the undrowned women
the hope floats women the strong
the water knows us
the whole-note women
the half-step harmony song

the fire frees us
the fast-ass women the fall-in-love women the freaks
the fire is full of the all-out women
the walk-out women the sweet
the fire is finding the love-lost women
the worth-it women the ones
fire is blazing the brash blues women
the black-eyed women
the wiry women with guns
the fire is becoming the sun

our work here is not done

spill

How She Knew

spill (v) 2. (of liquid) flow over the edge of its container. "Some of the wine spilled onto the floor."

SYNONYMS: overflow, flow, pour, run, slop, slosh, splash

she lit a candle for Tuesday. she lit a candle for sweat. she lit a candle when you woke up and the sheets were wet. she lit a candle for lovers. she lit a candle for friends. she lit a candle for maybe and for sometimes and for depends. she poured some water for cooling. she poured some water for sleep. she drank some water for the things she said she would do and forgot that week. she offered food to the corners and to the mourners and the ghosts. she planted grass for the exiles and the stateless and the hosts. she chanted peace to the pilgrims and the playmates and the pimps. she chewed on glass for the mothers and never even winced. she prostrated before the teacups and the teachers and the books.

and it is still it is still it is still

it is still just as bad as it looks.[1]

let the bathtub overflow with hot water and quilt pieces. let
the grit of everyday settle to sandbar. let the soap get lost in
love letters. soak out their lying blue blood. let the salt of the
tears she was saving and the sweat she used up scour her skin
like the tough love of black teachers. let porcelain become slate
against her back.

she doesn't care.

let it seep into her hair with the whispered blood of moontime.
let her hold her breath for now, submerge for evidence, eureka.
let her sink into the sum of wet mosaic over brown. immersed
in the material of what? what now?[2]

the same crunch the same stem the same sweet green wetness
again.

her heart is a pot full of greens to chew and swallow all the
nourishment she knows.

she used to salt it. overcook it. contaminate it with swine. she
used to leave it on the stove all day and forget it half the time.
she even cut it with molasses once and washed it down with
wine. why isn't love red like it should be. her growing heart.
ain't flesh and muscle like it could be.

just all that deep bright green.[3]

she thought she heard dogs barking. she knew she heard crows. she sensed a plague of locusts crowding her windows. she remembered how fast and choking ivy could grow. she expected poison sweets from the neighbors and toxic rain from above. anticipated anthrax in her laundry. awaited everything but love.

in her ears violence was biblical. in her eyelids lightning was fate. in her heart staying here one more moment was a fatal mistake. but attack in its historic signature requires all strings attached. so she continued baking the cookies. (convinced it would be her last batch.)[4]

there is a crawling part of every day. the part that doesn't leave the ground, slides under all the affirmations, bills paid, slips unshown, good girl status tentatively unshattered. there is part of the breathing that doesn't need that either, somewhere at the base of the lungs. steamship fuel that pushes on her day, the part of her that doesn't know how to walk with the full sensation of the particles on the floor, the dredge in the river, the dust of what happens in fake human heaven, the sense to want something else.[5]

whoever thought of an upside-down cake? her fingertips graze the razor can edge. the swimming pool pineapples float in sweet. *and the weight of the cake will crush them,* she thinks. *will grow dense fill the pan and crush them,* she knows. *like the heavier heaviness of days.* she absently slices her finger, adding red into the yellow, and cries. *and what did they ever do?* it hurts. *and what did they ever do?*[6]

was that her baby's skin? what water did. what waste. what fire
did. what thrown-away machine. could not be. this could not
be the smooth the kissed the cherished the Vaselined skin she
would scald her life off for. was this the sweetest face she had
sacrificed sleep and sense for? was this the child she brought
here? and why?

she did not cry. she did not touch. it was too much. the texture
of her loss.[7]

it's the center of her forehead. like someone stole the light and brought it back so bright it makes her dizzy. makes her skull grow cracked and break. makes her heartbeat halo heaven hardly breathe.

like the sun sought her out and shaped a laser just to clean out every decision she made. when she closes her eyes the walls of her brain are infrared and pulsing. someone is sounding the alarm. beating the bell of her brain. and all she can hear is *no*.[8]

it was a mirror. she thought it was a mirror. it had always been a mirror. but every now and then something wasn't right. something was in the mirror that wasn't back here. was that a book? a mug of tea? a paintbrush? how did they get there into her sight but out of her reach? and that woman. almost the same but eyes on fire, smile almost inviting. what *is* she doing with my only face?[9]

the photograph blurs black and white in her hand. the edges
are marked with the date like evidence. the image looks like
outer space the splotches like a gerbil astronaut. she wonders
has anyone been to the moon or to the inner reaches of a black
woman's womb. it could all be a trick of paper and eye, a race to
see who fakes it best.

the printout shines, bending her sweaty hands, reflecting her
fingernails, grooving into a slight indent. she needs a piece of
string. a miniature clothesline to hang this thing. a mobile to
turn it around. a terrestrial angle must be found. she feels like
she's floating away. and wonders if that's how she got this way.
being blurry and captured and small.

she turns the image upside down, holds it up to the ceiling,
drops it down on the ground and tries to walk down the hall.
her hands on her neck, she stands there until she falls and curls
her knees into her chest. is this the result of doing her best.
is this the leak of her love. or is this the self she is thinking of
when she cannot sleep at night. the tiny unstill life in black and
white. blurred glimpse of a dark held world. the technician had
looked for phallic signs and failed. so he said *it's a girl.*[10]

the first time i thought of you, you were swimming, towards you, through me. first time i thought i was drowning in a world that needed you in it or it would disappear. first time i knew you existed the rest of the history of the world popped like a bubble unready unworthy and my body wanted only future, only you. the first time i felt you move we were deep underwater under something built to keep us under and i couldn't see anything but I understood there was something above everything. above everything despite everything I would find fresh air and breathe again. above everything despite everything I would free you. my best idea yet.[11]

could they open her legs into scream, cut her belly open and
reach. can they do whatever they want to do to bring the baby
through the breach through the gap of what she knows and
what the kid is here to teach. does she matter? is it money at
her middle is it mystery or mud. is it meaning or mistake. is it
proof of passed-down blood? are her birthing hips a blessing
her bewildered brain a dud. what is she doing here? is she
waterwreck or witness is she push or hush or thud. when the
universe is opened will she last?[12]

was she dipped in paint. split open like achilles. where was she weak? she looked at her body and saw only pores, only wet spaces, vessel, opening. she was whole. was she. born or made. was she possible? she looked at her fingertips for a seam. pinched her skin in case it was all a dream. was she real? the new female being, first of her kind, couldn't believe herself.[13]

How She Spelled It

_____

spill (v) 3. (with reference to the contents of something) empty out or be emptied out onto a surface.

"Passengers' baggage had **spilled out** of the hold."

it actually lifts her out of the bed. breathing or something like it. water in her veins. salt. spirit. rush. she has no one to describe it to. she would say wave crash but she has not seen the ocean. would say lightning. would say wait and come back, i'll show you. the next day she draws it in flour on the floor, the stars she has seen with her body, the stars she holds, they are children. and the shapes she makes are the shapes of her hands in every direction. she doesn't have the word *fractal*, she is inside a kaleidoscope where color merges to nothing she has ever seen. flour on her dirt floor on her brown skin. the only thing bright enough to make it real.[1]

because she was a cave. papyrus. she was inventing a language. herself. she was lighting up the darkness. her skin. however dull, the person who holds the tool can say *i am not an animal.* can she? can say there is control. there is reason in what she feels. cannot. say that and be heard. she is not. an animal. so she brights it in the darkness. her skin. so she spells it in the tomb. her covered arms. her battered womb. she makes a place to right her walls again. she tilts and wields it expertly. her pain. the spell she scratches in her skin. her name.[2]

i am wrong. she told herself. *born wrong. or more like retrieved.*
walk wrong, talk wrong, even now. she grieved. *and who in the*
hell set things up like this? then she wrote it in the salt spilled
on the table. *wrong.* she wrote it in the flour on the floor. *wrong.*
she wrote it in chicken blood on the stump. and in grease on
the counter. and she circle dialed it rotary home to her mother.
and she postcard wrote it across to her sister. and she wrote
it on her own wrists with toothpaste that night and smeared
it over her teeth. and she bit herself wondering about sinews,
worrying about the palimpsest of veins. but in the end she was
too vain because when she spelled *wrong* in the steam in the
mirror it was not her name.[3]

she put the words in his breakfast. wiped the spoon with the
ink, stirred it deep into black tea. the words were blue and she
pressed them into the china saucer underneath his teacup the
delicate bowl before she put the oatmeal in. the words were
sins that she allowed herself in the morning. imagining they
would realign his brain rewrite his thoughts unstain her life.
the words were hearses. not curses. just designed to carry him
away. she named him what he was. so gentle he would swallow
it and not choke. her wrought written loops of language printed
careful on the whiteness sweet as poison. before the sugar and
the milk. she loved the soft blue ocean of wishing he would
die. burying it in the heavy oats. she imagined the blue of her
own bruises spreading daily on his insides until his muscles
could not take it and his bones grew weak and bent. she wrote
vitamin hate in his breakfast. receipt for how her life was
spent.[4]

she just took a corner of one piece of paper and scribbled in blue ink and loops what she meant. and then she folded it up and ate it. and then the next day she did it again. and after eight months she danced and looked you in the eye. and told you with her deep blue tongue that fiber could do wonders. and something was coming. she could say it with her gut and release it rather joyfully. and what do you know. we are all full of it now.[5]

first she would have to clear the table. put away the brightly
colored miscellany on the central surface of her lying life. first
she would have to admit the table was there before she was.
first she would have to sit at the table and watch relationships
fall apart and the table stay together. first she would have
to trust that a table can be strong enough for a question.
she would have to sit there wondering how a table got to be
stronger than her. she would have to move the kitchen table
to her office and meditate on that. how much love does wood
absorb. she would have to ask the oldest tree she knows. *how do
you turn paper into food?*[6]

she tied paper to her wrists with rubber bands, kissed ink and
sat down. pulled elastic over her ankles for what it meant.
eyelash staples broke and rusted daily off her face. collated
and cross. she referenced her elliptical contents monthly and
wondered, bent at the edge of her bed, how her thin-paged life,
her black-type days amounted to only this.[7]

she had thought to hold the question whole, with hairpins and her hands, until you got here. thought she could stay it with staples and standing still. surely housework could wait. surely heaven and handbasket would grant her a few moments to hold it together. after all her waiting, surely this. but surely is nothing and it fractured slowly, the question, in her patient mended heart until her bone remembered who to punish, broke away from her stoic knowing and began to stab small ventricles of trust. you didn't come home. and this was not eden. she smashed your chest of drawers to smithereens.[8]

she sands them out. the grooves they used to walk in. the steps they once stepped into. the time they wasted here. she sawdust saves them. the crooked mornings the creaking nightwalks. the pacing evenings. she smooths them out. redeeming something returning woodsign asking for heart pine to hear her out. she won't remember the routine wreckage she used to walk through barefoot here. she sands it out.[9]

a framed family picture is a phantom. it is a fountain of glass to cut her now. all this time believing that glass is water gets caught in her throat like the sanded-down future of what it is possible to say. she is so smooth now. disabused of how what is was supposed to look like. now that the pane is a million drops. now that she has dropped the frame of what she thought she was making onto the floor where bare feet sacrifice and smile.[10]

so she stood steeple-straight in the shards still in proud
shock of her quick work. the living room now rainbowed
glass collected on the floor, the mosaic of how mad she had
been. she almost laughed out loud but she was too breathless
at this room, more broken than she. no picture frame could
contain her now. she was prism reborn. she was sharp refracted
everything.[11]

not everybody knows my name, but everyone knows what I
taste like. salt after malt liquor. vault where the soul is kept.
everyone knows my sweat under their tongue when they try
to say free market. wet wild wick when they try to spark it on
the fourth of july again. mildew of what I do for you. everyone
knows the bloom of the brackish floor of the living room
America. i taste like hysteria sedated with a case of blues. i
taste metallic like tap shoes Morse coding no. i taste like dirty
city snow that can't stay white. i taste like your morning breath
after waking up all night afraid your stuff is gone. i taste like
sparrow song and hunger, taste like blackened coal mined
lungs. i taste like military blunders limping up and down the
street. i taste like used rag fermentation that gets used again
another week. can i speak?[12]

How She Left

---

spill (v) 4. (of a number of people) move out of somewhere quickly.

"Students began to spill out of the building."

SYNONYMS: stream, pour, surge, swarm, flood, throng, crowd

it shows up on Saturday. purple and loud. tender as a plum and just in time for visitors. it shows up on Sunday red sea of vanity. veins and tributaries unreadying church. it shows up on Monday gray unprofessional routine, relentless and ready to work. it shows up on Tuesday totally unforgiveable immune now to Advil interpreted as shirk. it shows up on Wednesday evolving and ashy from all the concealer attempted to cloak. it shows up on Thursday with flowers and candy and jewelry and liquor to make it a joke. it shows up on Friday but she can't see it. she can't see it. it shows up on Friday but she can't see it. she walked out the door over mirrors she broke.[1]

she could breathe. that much. she could breathe. and maybe
her ribs felt it too much but it was there. and she had to believe
that the network of microscopic balloon cells in her chest had
a say and could collaborate with oxygen to make some small
decision called live. she had more to give, she decided, as smoke
ran the distance of her blood. telling her she should walk
more she should breathe more deeply she should cherish crisp
presence over warmth. she was smiling as a breeze brushed
her cheek like a matte page out of a fall catalog full of plaid she
could not now or never before afford. and her eyes watered
like this. like an ancestor kiss. and the laughter crackled out
from the embers of her red engine heart and she laughed and
laughed at her lesson. what an early winter wonder that it took
burning the whole damn house down to find out.[2]

no one took a photograph but I see her. one foot on a lower step, one still on the porch. looking behind her, hands gripping the newest definition of what her hands could carry. her elbow points towards the still where moonshine and her man will drown their disbelief later in a proof so strong you'd think it would be clean. but she is a witness, it is simply mean. fermenting as it has been under their bed and freezing the synapses in her head until now. if she could keep this posture she wouldn't trade it for all the hurried motions just before nor the years she hustled around trying to convince that man she was a person, a soft place, an asset, something other than a drum for his drunk tantrum nights and increasing afternoons. she kept the spoon and tied to it the cleanest sheet and wrapped it around the last of the dried meat and the bread she had baked her decision in. as the bread rose she filled out her skin and her body got soft and got full again and her bones said this house would not win she was free she was getting out.[3]

she decided to walk out the door barefoot, hands empty unburdened by everything she had broken. she decided to weigh exactly as much as she weighed plus one thin favorite dress. she left the door open, screen and everything. she didn't take key nor pocket change. she didn't write a note or expect to call. she didn't expect anything at all. she stepped one at a time closer to the horizon using those empty hands to shade her face from the sun when it blocked her way.

she decided to stay and clean up everything. almost as if nothing had ever happened and never would. she put cinnamon and water in the oven so it would seem like she had been true and domestic the whole time. never mind there would be nothing to show. appearance is usually enough she remembered and dug her nicest dress out of the trunk and wore the shoes that pinched. and sat by the window while the cinnamon replaced the salt and waited.

she decided to paint her discontent all over the outside walls with leftover house paint and chicken feathers and grease. she decided to pull up all the flowers that were not purple enough for how she felt. she decided to throw rocks in a cross formation warning any sacrificial company to stay the fuck away. she decided all that and then sat down and wrote about it instead.

she decided to call her sister and then her cousin and then her sometime friend. she decided to call the pastor at the church she went to once around the bend. she decided to call her mother and sugarcoat everything but the worst. she decided to call her grandparents long-distance via hearse. she decided to call on Jesus but figured he might not remember her name. she decided to call on the talking drum but her hands were curled up in shame. she decided to call up everyone but figured they weren't at home. so she walked out the door to see where they were and that's how she started to roam.[4]

she tripped halfway down the porch steps before she felt it.
mother deep smothering her ankles. round, locked, growing
hot to the untouched. VapoRub tingle to the flesh. *what would*
her mother say. and right there her wild skip turned shuffle
like trying on cheap shoes bound by plastic. *if the shoe fits*, her
mother would have sung. and she had never said mama no they
don't fit and her mother never wore flat shoes anyway nor did
she raise her eyes long or far enough to escape. nor did she raise
our shero to be ungrateful for the story she almost fit into. but
hero is not heroine and neither the shoes nor the dress nor
the damn panties ever fit right and somewhere there was sky
to suit her, sand to shape her, and an ocean to savor. so she
stomped three times as if to unshackle somebody and stepped
deliberately off.[5]

can I say sometimes the mother was glad about the distance
and the unreliable post and the prejudice of telegraph
companies and the constant smell of the roast. can I say she
felt relieved by what she couldn't have known (since she and
the farmer never upgraded to install a rotary phone). can you
tell she avoided the corner store and the gossips and the seers
and the well-connected minister and the questions of her peers.
you can imagine she bit her nails anyway while she untaught
herself to read and imagined that if she worked day and night
her conscience would be freed. but daughter's heartbeat
inescapable stole the piece of her pulse that was true. and that's
why when she was cleaning the window she noticed the dove as
it flew. when her youngest daughter finally escaped she smiled
to herself. she knew.[6]

For Harriet Tubman

this can never be equal to this. every way she set the table.
every form of rice she put on the other side of sugar, every
stitch through cotton and the numbness of her fingertips.
nothing is not even equal to nothing. knowing is not equal to
no. so she renamed herself after her mother, left her dirtbag
husband, looked up at her north star god and said "let's go."[7]

the walls want her. they are telling her something. the wood pattern on the floor is dancing. move. could her skin burn out the truth or would she need the release of stomach acid to let go what she never should have had to know. this chair is sharp and wrong and bruising. the ceiling is melting. get up. is her brain boiling up a remedy or a riddle. how many lightbulbs does it take to change a black girl. what cumulative caloric steam of sugarcane stolen rice, new jewel cinnamon and nutmeg. what oracular fever. this hot rice pudding is trying to tell her something. drop the spoon, girl. run.[8]

they thought it was just a tic. the way she kept her hands closed in shaking fists most of the day if she wasn't holding something. the way she was always holding something even if it turned out to be only air. they didn't watch closely enough to see the burned fingertips from the steam escaping from her palms. they just knew the silverware and dishes were brighter from her touch. the windows clearer, the countertops worthy of narcissus's doom. which is what they were living. they only had a sense for the vaguest reflection of themselves and the fulfillment of their laziest wishes. it was no superpower that made her invisible to them, that made it possible for her to move from room to room without them knowing her sequence. they just didn't care how their world was made clean, since their minds remained shrouded in grime.

she, however, had no tolerance for slime. and it may have been the swamp women, the hot springs women, the first cave women, the core-of-the-earth women, the salt, that gave her what she had. we don't know where it came from. we just know when that white bastard tried to put his spunk on her he wound up with a third-degree burnt-up member, steam shriveled into nothing, question marks for his generations. because she had no fingerprints and she was gone.[9]

the grail was in the pantry next to grain alcohol and cornmeal. if they wanted to find it they could have asked her anytime. but the pastor never asked her anything and in fact the way he looked at us in the churchyard you would have thought he was thinking we lived on mars and grazed on blue grass. the grail was there. too high for her to reach, and safe.

the divine dust was everywhere and for shame she had been trying to sweep it up for years before she realized it was that pulverized god that kept her wood floors and plaster mantels from getting clean.

the milagros are in the basement, she is sure of it. the body parts of other women hung like smokehouse family. a warning. what god would want a sacrifice like that? she had to leave.[10]

they called her peanut. not for carver. not for the etched inventiveness she ground down into. not for cut. for cute.

they called her peanut. tiny. edible. they were not referring to the roughmap shell, the space she shrunk between, the armor that protected her from everyday uncle-type hell and her smooth skin. they were not naming the split-able sin of her seed prove double groove, her legume legroom. they did not know how much they needed her name in order to claim their own too-wide masculinity over her child-bride sensitivity. they could barely see her. but she could be butter, she could be fuel, she could be clock workings or gruel, she was that flexible. her name inexorable in the mouths of the barely knowing, received right when her mama started showing, she heard it that early. and she was sweet, not surly, smooth, not chunky, graceful, not clunky. she was who they imagined they needed her to be, with a smile, not a frown. and when she escaped she was fully free. and that's how she would always be. her nickname changed to *nutcase. no-name. that crazy bitch.* they had no way to track her down.[11]

How She Survived until Then

---

noun
noun: **spill**; plural noun: **spills**
a quantity of liquid that has spilled or been spilled.
"a 25-ton oil spill"

an instance of a liquid spilling or being spilled.
"He was absolved from any blame for the oil spill."

SYNONYMS: spillage, leak, leakage, overflow, flood

maybe it was her mother for her coat-hanger nettle tea free
arrival on the planet. maybe it was her father for staying home
at night for once. who knows? maybe it was the god of Abraham
for not thinking about daughters. maybe it was that bush she
fell into for not being rose or burning. maybe it was her siblings
leaving food for her in her slowness. maybe it was the soda
jerk for looking the other way. maybe it was the schoolteacher
for making her clean all the chalkboards. maybe it was the
teacher's pet for not making her stay. maybe it was the crossing
guard for staying ten minutes extra. maybe it was the trees for
making her green skirt blend in. maybe it was pastor himself
always trying to seem so free of sin. maybe it was the murderer
himself for thinking boys are better prey. maybe it was her
strong ankles from that brief stint at ballet. maybe it was all
thanks to ma'dear for constantly making her pray. maybe it was
the echo on the sidewalk for having something to say. maybe
it was inherited swiftness in her legs that let her run home
that day. but the boogeyman didn't quite catch her. so thanks.
either way.[1]

she grew tall in the middle of a large family. forest thick
with tangled roots. trained on how gently you could step on
everyone's feet. stretch marks on her neck from reaching
through that nappy canopy for sky. one day she started to feel
that her bones knew each other too well, stacked as they were
from sharing the bed, wearing the worn-out clothes, rubbing
the relative shoulder. when she reached she was already looped
through the crook of a sister the nape of a brother the shared
sweat of siblings in the carbon dioxide heat. not organism
but ecosystem in the loudest house on the street. and if you
stopped to think, someone was singing along. and if you sought
the corner, someone was dancing to the song. and if you needed
a moment the moment was already gone and dinner was
ready and don't dare dawdle long, there are no seconds. so she
reckoned when the chance came to go away she would be okay.
or it seems so from that look we sometimes find on her face.
when the chance came all she could see with her skin was space
space space space space.[2]

she doesn't remember the first time she landlocked cursed.
maybe it was the wet in the voice of an uncle, not a sailor but
in love with his boat of a car. he had no legs for land, she could
tell that. maybe it was the oil dirty words he used to talk about
the Cadillac that she knew were mouthsize love, public but
unknowable, intimate for all to jealous see. she whispered to
make her mouth her own, thinking these were things that
her mother would not say, this was how she could change
the content and the shape of her face, not just the order and
arrangement of her resignation. and around her small friends
she felt grown in the tongue like a person who knew things
that she had no way to know. and in church she felt guilty
and repented every week. she was playing prophet to her own
scandalous adulthood, she was praying for it, calling it forth
like her girl future could be slick, like she would slide through
days uninhibited into the next. but she was wrong. curse on
her lips notwithstanding she could not escape the rhythm of
traction and sand of creating the world every day with her
hands just like the women her uncle gas-tank-sailed away from.
she could have spit, but she just sucked her teeth.[3]

she is learning it slowly cell by cell. the prison breathing that
will save her. she is painting her skin the color of walls with
prayers she thinks she is making up. the same prayers her
bright ancestors carried to Brazil, whispersong shared to battle
enslavement. *may they not see me. may they not hear me. may
they not smell me. may they not feel wind and think of me. may
they forget my very name.* it is not quite complete, the spell she
is spinning around herself. when she walks home from the store
the boys still see enough to harass her. but most days it seems
to have worked perfectly on her teacher. for better or worse. day
in day out. she act like she don't even know she there.[4]

she paid attention if not dues. she knew about weakness from her own scarred knees. she knew. she listened under the skin of the respondents, the crested heartbeats of the rich. she knew when to say it. between the pulses of the other preteens who didn't have to swim with sharks. she knew to thicken her own skin. sharpen her smiling teeth. insert the joke into their craws so suddenly they could not breathe. their braced mouths could not close. their erstwhile friends let go their lungs and laughed out all the hallway air. this was how she took the tank of middle school. this was how. otherwise she couldn't have. it would never have been fair.[5]

she drew her letters on with eyeliner. a straight line was not a bruise. a shadowed eye was not black. a penciled arch was innocence, not bewilderment, not desperation. she would draw the face she wanted. and then wear it. yes she would.[6]

she kept some under the table and in the back of the china cabinet. she kept the vacuum switched to reverse for how they gasped about nothing. she conserved it with her own shallow breathing, her own holding it in, her only corseted emotions, her smile. she baked some into pastry puffs and blew furtively towards the children's rooms. she moved the plants three inches back from where they usually presided. she knew if there were ever to be enough she would have to provide it, save it, hide it. air. for when the company was gone.[7]

some days she put her hands on her belly and pushed. she held
the roundness of air and muscle like it was the earth itself.
she shaped the mostly water like it was the blue of birds and
baby clothes. this was what she wanted. years went by and she
started to mark the walls with imagined heights. throw rice
on the floor where the footsteps would have been scattered
around her skirts, the child who would have loved her. and then
her hand would shape the roundness of a head coming up to
her knee, then her waist. brave bright curl protected brain. the
future that would have mercy on her. she put candy at the door
and poured honey into the river to show the house the land
itself how sweet a mother she could have been. and only when
the dreamchild grew taller than her could she look at the sky
without resentment.[8]

the center of the bed got so low you'd think the springs would have met the floor that summer. by fall it was all she could do to climb out, take some time out everyday to rebuild her back strength. but the mattress and the floor never touched each other and it was not because of the strength of any bone or wooden frame. it was the sad magnet under the bed that drew her into the scary place, the dark place of needing that pit of the stomach feeling more than she needed to be free.[9]

she is biting her nails again. some story about where she ends even as dead skin steels itself strong and something else. she is pulling out her hair again thinking there must be a limit to the cloud of secrets growing out. she is skin or so she thinks again. she is bone or so the floorboards tell her. she is fat and all the old ones smile because it will not protect her from what she knows. the difference between sunlight and her face is only scale. the difference between her mouth and music is starting and stopping. the difference between her hands and stars is proximity to the window. the difference between earth and her sweet brown skin is not so much now that she blinks about it. she is eating dirt again. preparing.[10]

leaning in she is almost top-heavy with brain and untwisted braids and worry. breathing in she smooths the ocean of her forehead. breathing out her eyebrows probably drown. hand behind her own back she reaches for her leg for her strength her other hand. keep breathing. muscles enter stretch and shoulder wisdom pop unlocks. her feet root legs remember what it takes to stand. there is always something to reach across always something to hold on to. even if it's your own wilding body even if it is your own hand.[11]

sugar bit tractor beam refrigerator door at night. sure. she moves towards the light. moth pantomime without the flame plug-in nightlight shadow game. indeed. she is afraid of dark. blemish kit bleaching cream wide brim hat at noon. true. lighter lighter still. the truth the Jesus march the light the skirt restrained and hair done right. amen. the Lysoled floor the kitchen bright the hands dried out from scrubbing. right. her pride and joy. the light eyes of the neighborhood on boys with hair that's twice as good. duly noted and doted upon. but that renegade, that open threat, that sweat that hasn't happened yet, that bold harbinger of regret, the sun, he calls her out.

with memories of muscles taught to tear themselves and grow. with sunspot fairy leaf branch glow. with edges turning back at noon as sisters speak with clouds. or jumping in the creek with giggled ripples twice as loud. with knowing that her blood could heat the rest of blackened days. with heat-drunk porch-sunk lemonade haze. the recklessness of resting after basking in his gaze. the sun. he calls her out.

so pretending to mind the zinnias. pretending to polish the windows from outside. pretending to look for the children. pretending to gossip about bimbos. pretending to need some air. pretending that it will be rare. pretending to sweep the porch. she rebrowns her spirit. scorched.[12]

her fingers rake the dirt pull the roots eat the hurt under her nails. enter earthworm. enter snails. center trails laid by the sweetest decomposers. cue the music start the rain press the chest in to stain the housedress half-life. hold the trowel hold the hoe hold the spade this will be played out by hand now. heap the heartache heap the tears pour the solitary years into the land now. grind the gristle round the womb compost tomb best hope and channel to rebirth now. kiss the limestone grasp the shells sweat your song into the well groundwater heavy. pray for lightning push for loud, hone in on rainstatic radio shroud and sound like summer. wind is the drummer cymbal through remember everything you do becoming flowers. becoming squash becoming fern. remember everything you learn will soon out-green you. remember. everything you forget will grow.[13]

What She Did Not Say

spill (v) *informal*
reveal (confidential information) to someone.
"He was reluctant to spill her address."

SYNONYMS: reveal, disclose, divulge, blurt out, babble,
betray, tell, blab

"He's spilling out his troubles to her."

For Phillis Wheatley

sits facing pane wondering who will vouch for black ink shaped by her deep-lined hands brown as oak and interlaced now. and who will be a witness and what drum call remember. the sound of her writing is the quietest dance made to tiptoe over ocean. tree floor drum trunk may you reach. mother tilt back west and hear me.[1]

she puts her hand on her heart, fingers spread past allegiance. and whose hand dance does she reprise with her ungraspable fear. the will to live is more than holding on to bones that betray us. her will to live bequeathed by dead women she holds her heart she cannot hold her hot to the touch heart oh uncontainable heart where are my mothers how how how could you leave me here?[2]

who sent you? who spent your childhood up with barefoot errands? who beat you? who shaped your face down like that to cheekbone and chin? who fed you sugar like it was love? who told you your dreams were not good enough to sit on? who trained you to bite your own tongue? who reminded you of a river that wanted you to move when you were looking for the ocean all the time? who said you were not their favorite song, just the song that happened to be on, that they could not turn off lest they remember their own silence? who gave you ambition, not because they believed in you but because you could not believe in their version enough? who stared when you needed tears and blinked when you needed a window? who pushed you into the world so bent? who sent you here so broken?[3]

everything was so smooth. the way they sliced their sentences with words sharpened at home. she wondered if they salted all conversation or whether these were preserved pronouncements they wished they could have said to the husbands who coolly cut them down behind closed doors. she almost had to admire their art. the way they could make their wasted lives match a new dress while insulting yours and sounding so sweet. how their daily daggers refracted off of tea services like prisms. how their tears must have been like diamonds, bright and only really able to cut each other.[4]

she spells it in spilled oatmeal and salt over her shoulder to catch the footprints. she writes it backwards in the steam may it depart from her lungs. she taps its rhythm with her houseshoes on. may it unhand her heart, may it let go her children, may it run. she sits with the syllables surrounding her, embracing her unfit throat. she envies the peacocks their shrieking. she won't offer one whole note. she flicks Morse code off her fingers and tries not to blink out the light. she cannot say what he will do to her, but she can, notwithstanding, fight.[5]

you are shrinking in your sleep. your stacked shoulders. your
bone grinding against itself. you wake up and there is less
frame to you. less space on which to hang your ragged name.

i thought it was your dream quality or your vitamin d, but in
truth, it is the days you turn your back on into shrug. a drug.
the way you betray everything you learn. it is not what i feed
you. if people knew they would think it was poison, the way you
sleep all night and wake up more or less the same.[6]

you set the table. so lie in it. kneel on it. make space in between the central carcass and the forks that will stab you. you know what you did.

you built the table. dismantle it. break it down into sections or two-by-fours or splinters to remind how few times we ever sat here together.

you planted the tree. nappy roots and everything and all the fights your parents had reborn in leafy glory up the floorboards in my house.

you cut the tree down when it was mine to kill.

you dirt. you hurt me. hear about it.

you bang. you big fool. fly.[7]

they stared at each other starved long enough to know you cannot eat hate hate will eat you fast as it wants to. as soon as you wake up each day late. love lets you plant it tend it and water it at twilight and spray and stay and every day they kept deciding what to do with every day. so every day they decided one more day hungry would be okay. and every day each one waited for the other one to say:

i was wrong i was wrong it has been too long this is my song to your endurance i want to belong i want to be strong and together we can do it i was wrong about thinking that you were wrong i was wrong to put us through this

and when their mouths didn't have osmosis left to water and their eyes didn't have oceans left to offer and their skin didn't have any death to grow their hair with and their voices which they never used could have only been shrill they admitted to themselves what they loved more than love, or each other:

will.[8]

how did you get here? what trumped-up troupe of slave-ship
sloop put you here on my doorstep in your nastiness. who told
you this was the place to get in someone's face and act like
you could pry between the rock-hard place lean-to i mean to
protect. who put the swivel in your neck that you could use two
faces against me in two different places you know not what you
are. who lent you their car so you could drive a wedge between
the ledge i stand on and my need. how you get the gas the gall
and the speed to show up here of all places?[9]

there is the fault line that started when her heel hit the front walk. the former molten edge of the world. there is the fracture that moved down from where he punched the wall to the foundation. there are the weak points in the wood from the children running in place. there are the cracks from where we all been absentmindedly eating the paint. there is the corner swelling of our backs against the wall. point being, don't blame me when this house falls.[10]

you will know me by the curling iron burn inside my thigh,
by the scattered shrunken sky when you look at me. you will
know me by the insurance that you took out on my trust. by the
tarnish and the rust in my eyes for you. you will know me by
the scuff on the bottom of my heart which was new when you
found it and is weary. you will know the me you made, damaged
and afraid if you find me again. that's my theory.

i will know you by the fat I have landed on your legs, lush
from no longer lifting your dreams. i will know you by the only
clothes you have left to wear which all got my fingerprints
up and down the seams. i will know you by the sound of your
unearned breath and the love and time you stole. i will know
the you i made by letting you unmake me. and i will run the
other way. that's my goal.

they will know us by the shadow we cast over sunrise, the
horizon we can't ever fill. they will know us by the emptiness
under our ankles, the float of our skirts, by the thrill. they will
know us by the way we glance at them sideways anticipating
the hit. they will know where we're from by what we'll do to not
go back there. and they will take us or leave us. that's it.[11]

What He Was Thinking

---

spill (n)
2. a fall from a horse or bicycle.
"Granddad took a spill while riding the bay mare."

SYNONYMS: fall, tumble

(v) cause (someone) to fall off a horse or bicycle.
"The horse was wrenched off course, spilling his rider."

SYNONYMS: unseat, throw, dislodge, unhorse
"The horse spilled its rider"

Hear the chainsaw laughter. Hear the tree-killing parking lot laughter. Hear the smoked-away resistance. Hear the tar stuck the choking laughter. Hear the domino razor's-edge laughter. Hear the scratch ma's good table and destroy food forever laughter laughter. Hear the sound that made her stop caring. Hear the overworked husband ridicule his wife with all the homeboys staring. Hear the cut through rings and sap and everything laugher laughter laughter. Hear the dreams of our mother fall to the floor and never get raised up after.[1]

there is a crack. is it the sky opening. is it the crowd awakening. is it the bleachers shaking. is it the cheerleaders breaking their ribs. or is it his neck. is it god asking for skull? his skill is not asking about it not waiting for it not saving a drop of it. his value is in his waived rights his offered flesh his sacrifice.

the body is more than a case for the brain. it is a vessel for the game. it is a hall of pain it is an owner who owes you the honor of loaning you a shirt that says property of the team, it is neon green sweat and abandon you drink up and think it's love.

but there is a crack. is that the ceiling or the pavement. give me Astroturf to lie down on forever. is that sunlight or stadium light. i am levitating tonight. coach said leave it all on the field right? am i smiling? forgive me. forgive me all of you. i know not what breaks through.[2]

it was a training hologram. shadow art. that was what he told himself the first time. it was a phantasm. visual echo of the dim blue in his grandfather's down-looking eyes. it was the myth that had kept them almost men. it could not. could not still be real.

it was a joke. must be. they said the state didn't even walk around no more. let alone wear blue. they said it would let us alone now that the sidewalks were theoretical.

but despite all his improvised limberness, all his fastfooted faith, he was cornered and he felt it. a hinge in his neck go out, dream in his eye go dark.[3]

she could feel it at school. certainly at the bus stop. continually on the street. three breaths away from it on her own front porch. the red. laserbeam mosquito around her shoulders, brand grazing her leg, government-issued stamp invalidating flesh as the house of any spirit, any worthwhile scream.[4]

the rev was louder than her heart. the hot fuel circulatory
system more beloved more known by the men in her
neighborhood than anything she could say or feel. the bass
more beckoning than the drum of her walk. she walked around
whispering *vroom*. she moved her hands clockwise with her talk.
the men she knew might have wanted to go to medical school.
but that was not an option. so they became freelance surgeons
for cars. and their curbside manner was so graceful she could
cry. it was teaching her something about love and slavery. the
little boys ran home from school to get grease on their faces.
she stomped her pumps on the brake side but nobody noticed.
she watched them willing tending tending tending towards
machines.[5]

he had one of those real round black jazz musician names.
coleman. hargrove. something that let you know he was deep
and loved by the land. that he was diamond but still dark.
that even if he was lightskinned he had soul. you could trust a
person like that to steal everything. the song out of your head.
the salt out of your shimmy. the white out of your rice and the
sun out of your stomach.

type of man make you hungry but you ate and are eating. dig
though you thought you were deep already. it was his name
they wanted and never got. they had enough pieces of him, skin
cells on the sheets, hair in the sink, fingernails in their own
flesh to make another him if they needed to, but not the name.
he would not claim them in the morning he just owned them
for the night. so they learned to write early in the sunrise hour
when he left.

they learned hieroglyphics and calligraphies of neglect. they
were afraid to go to sleep and wake up so bereft. because
that early morning clarity is what you are afraid to know and
somewhere in it was the key (b flat) to why he had to go.[6]

was it a coat? was it a top coat of egg yolks and yesterday's flour that gave her shine and grit at the same time. was it the swamp. was it the thickness of the air that made her never naked always forcefield fortified. was it the clothes and how they didn't even touch her skin or dare to. was it the dust in here and how it spelled her name like glitter. was it the salt, the tears, the trade, the test, the tuning that made me want to wash her clean?⁷

it was about air. it was about not needing to breathe in again if that was what it took. it was requiring neither brushed teeth nor words formulated to move in close. it was about how many times. it was about how many times he had zoomed in on her face in his mind and tried to climb in the pores. it was about dogfights and nights still drinking because numb was shaking. it was about the same sad thing unsaid across generations of fathers known and unknown. it was about a brightness in his skin that beckoned hate. it was about the emptiness of the food he ate. it was about air and how she changed it. claimed it. shit. she drove him to it. she dared. she dared to breathe.[8]

how. how many. how many left. how many years left. how many years left open. how many years left open so. how many years left open so you. how many years left open so you could. how many years left open so you could walk out.

when. when did. when i did. when did i eat. my when did i eat. when did i eat my way. when did i eat my way through. when did i eat my way through this. when did i eat my way through this table.

where. where does. where love does. where does love go. where does love go when. where does it go when love. where does love go when it runs. where does love run when it goes away.

who. who knows. who knows how. who knows how to. who knows how to stand.
whoever knows how to stand right. who knows how to stand right here whoever you are.

why. why now. why stay now. why stay now. why stay broke now. why stay now trust broke. why stay now that trust broke us.

what. what call. what call back. what call break back. what break would call you back.

if what. if you. if you go. what if you go.

because. because i. because i forgot.

to count.[9]

first comes the yawn. then the salt for the tears. then the
contraction in the womb that has been frozen for years. then
eyes still open, then blinking off fear, she realizes what she
has done. and your mouth opens too, to say what you have
said, to say what has worked before to claim back the tempo
that derails her temper and restarts the tempest in the August
house. you wait for the echo off the wall of your spouse, but
somehow the yawn mutes you. unsuits you. sits you back down.
first comes the yawn. then the salt for the tears. when she turns
around laughter is all that you hear. then your throat closes
into something like fear. she finally doesn't care.[10]

his pants actually fell down. the belt in his hand less powerful than the laughter in her eyes. *What. You gone shuffle after me with your ankles like that?* and he knew in one blink that fear was not respect. it was what was left over when love done left. she had been tired, trapped, exasperated, beside herself, but never cowed. she had been bruised up broke and broken but she had never bowed.[11]

Except you ain't seen the county line. Except you ain't got no shoes, they mine. Except you ain't got nothing to lose, you fine. Except you ain't.

Except you wont born with but half a brain. Except you home training rougher than unthreshed grain. Except you better off staying and taking the strain. Except you won't.

Except you know exactly what mama would say. Except not having no daddy's making you act this way. Except you already wasted half of the day. Except half is not all at all.

Except you and your sins set it up for the fall. Except the sun is too big, the horizon's too tall. Except your will is too puny, your drive is too small. Less you do it.[12]

the time she shut the door and locked it. the time she walked to the edge, jumped off. the time she peed on the four-leaf clover. the time she let the peaches rot. the time she saved the kittens from drowning. the time she put out the trash and it went. the time she gave money out her hand to a beggar. the time she stamped the letter and got it sent. the time she burned your name into the doorway. the time she came home and broke down the door. the time she ate glass and her lips stayed unshattered. the time you asked her what she wanted and she said it

more.[13]

Where She Ended Up

---

spill (v)
let (wind) out of a sail, typically by slackening the sheets.

the motel vacancy sign knows its own code. morse. hoarse with
its own business. it is not firefly. this is not a rhythm to dance
to or a scatter to shake salt at, but she does both. cleaning
the temporary doorway, her own new threshold. no bread. no
broom. the sun is one storyteller drawing out sweat tracks,
focusing eyes. but at night the moon is clouded by the buildings
here and the darkness grows belligerent. this overworked neon
incident is teaching her something. what?[1]

she has her mostly empty purse and the uncomfortable shoes she left in. she has her chipped nails and her week ago done hair. she has her cracked compact and her wooden nickels. she has the cleft in her chin. she has her skin healing again. she has the scar on her shin that she got when she was six and didn't know that not all hurt is accidental. she has her shoulders tense but floating down with each breath. she has her lips tender and full of blood. she has her heart still pumping. it is quiet here and she can hear it. perhaps that really is enough.[2]

she gets round. she gets found out to be like the rest of them. fertile hurdle. she gets hounded about what she's gonna do. she gets sound. she gets teeth sucks and whispers whirlwinding around her. she gets slow. she gets slowmotion planet tilted and she can hear.

what she knows fits in the shape her hands make on her belly. it grows and the world can't shut her out. when she shows, eyeblinks measure the size of her problem. what she knows is not a solution but a route. when she adds she carries the one that shouldn't be sheltered. when she walks she divides the sidewalk into yes and know. when she stops the sky opens up and the ground prepares. when she dances the oldest folks smile and whisper "you glow."

and the young folks stare and the white folks pass quickly but glare sideways. which is fair. because she is going to have a sun. not gender but starburst she carries the one. and will burn up the boxes that shame, claim, and shun her for being. for freeing a certain set of cells into a certain hell that forgot it was heaven. and by month seven there is nothing you can say that contradicts the sway of how we get here every day and how we shine and how we stay. rising leavened.

when you see her dancing by, perceive her, leave her to her journey, breathe her, take a moment of gratitude to know that we achieved her.

and she doesn't have to say who the father is either.[3]

she stopped small talk. she made her mouth wide. that small pursed polite pause was for another life. she had outgrown it and she couldn't go back. and that was why she hated going to things like this where the talk was set on the small intent to not shatter the glass elephants around the room (with their jagged tusks). do not reveal or ask too much. we do not love here. we do not live here. we just make new deals consistent with our old one with the devil never to feel. we keep it neat. the loud yes and the belly laugh are for the street. we gave it up to shave the new growth from our lives from around our ears from behind our eyes. we slave it up to show how worthy we are. we are saving up for a freedom we will be unfit for when we get there. we have reined in our hair. the least you can do is swallow your mouth.

but that was not at all why she had come back to the south. and the moon in her. the freedom-better-be-this-or-it-better-be-soon in her. the glare-of-the-silver-spoon in her would not comply. would not shrink down and would not lie. so when she asked her brazen question she heard the forks drop but not the sigh.[4]

lord don't make this bathtub overflow with afterglow. my
downstairs neighbors may have prayed for rain or something
else to stop my pacing but at this point my racing heart
don't know how not to scream about this. a grown woman
baptized in her own hands is supermarket reading material
extraterrestrial waterbirth evidence that stranger though I
get, I am known inside myself. a deep space black of waiting
stars floats beneath a galaxy of soap. if someone asks i'll say
I slipped and hit my head on heaven. my hand phoned home.
not between lovers in this in-between space but between
the celestial folds the abundant grace of the base of my own
heavenly body. oh. one small step for the first kind. nobody
better come in here but me but if somebody asks I will softly
explain that years are not measured by light they are measured
by water. and I am wet as I want to be and was eve made the
flood and how great. praise the mother of opposable thumbs.[5]

she drug that treasure out the ocean with her shoreline slow drag. with her see-line pantyhose. with those legs. see her dress first flapping in wind then heavy with sea. and like the waves erasing drawings of sand revising mosaics of shell washing clean the unimaginable silt of getting here, she walked a different horizon. you could tell.

and the ghosts that landed there again again again again appreciated it just as well as the boys and the girls, the half-scandalized parents and the sand and the salt and the shells.[6]

on her back she can see everything. how the trees double-cross each other and survive. how branches open their smaller and smaller hearts into ever-reaching hands. how the birds pretend that they're not staying. she can see what the air isn't saying about stretch about need and the sky. about fragmentation conditions and needing to be high. all of this all of this just for the sun. all of this alone for the crucial hot one. so cruel and so far away that we live off her love and usually don't even burn.[7]

breathe. she extended her fingers, threw back her head, lowered
her shoulders. some days she could lean back into the flow
like it was a chair in her living room. safe, held, profoundly
understood. *how did the universe teach itself to love me so right*?
she laughed and the ripples reached everyone. some people felt
it in their shoulders and did a shimmy, some people felt in their
guts and excused themselves. children danced or had to pee.
when she breathed her people felt free.[8]

it was the girls and the way they needed silver. needed broken. needed crushed bright confetti from their foreheads to their toes. it was the shattered glass in them, the unstreetlit night. it was the fallen disco ball. it was the way they invited futures with different angles, prismatic possibilities. it was the way they funhoused mirrors. teenaged. showing up so different from the children we had raised.[9]

she sleeps in airplanes and dreams she can breathe clouds. dreams she can walk on what people think of her dreams. she no longer needs the ground. at night she looks down at the lights and knows they will eventually all go out and will she remember? will she know how to fly then?[10]

meditation? check. tea and oatmeal? check. writing exercise? check. mantra in the name of the mothers? check. stretching? check. slightly scenic walking? check. being love. being flight. being all of it. being light. being free. being loved for it. being table. being tree. being generational degree. being water. being dirt. being sun daughter. all three?

she's off. we'll have to get back to you.[11]

it was the water showing off. it was the sun dissolved to glitter. it was too scenic for him to mean anything he said. it could have been stunted transplant grass and sandtraps but even she wasn't invited to golf. so it was this. a river view in the middle of the day that made evening gown wearers forget their names and negotiators daydream. it was a Mississippi-specific scheme transplantable to Nile or Tigris or Jordan. some rivers seem too pretty to be heavy as they are. you never imagine a child turning to sludge at the bottom. a machine around some baby's neck. you can even forget the depths of what you know hypnotized by the dance of light in daytime. disremember what a mud-brown sister was sent to do. beware the shine of the surface the bright smile of suit. this river slick enough to drown me and you.[12]

you had me at hell no. and could have taken over. only i believed the space-time continuum couldn't hold as much of me as i was able to accept. especially not in multiple bodies. especially not through you (looking exactly like i had dreamt you up). i was afraid of dying. i was afraid of becoming God. it was the seventh day. and i refused to rest. and i refused to say that it was good.

she looked at herself in the mirror and all over the dance floor and flashing on the tv and wondered how did i spill. how did i spill out everywhere?[13]

she wonders if foundation is more than mud. how to free
her face from the dirt she does. she wonders if it comes from
someone's grave, if Maybelline is maybe the dust of slaves. she
remembers the first war that painted her this way to protect
her dimples and smooth her play. now she puts the mask on
every day to fill in her wrinkles, resentment, and rage. now she
browns up every day so her face is a stranger and her life is a
stage. now she thinks she was born this way. cheeks swept of
rebellion, eyes struck with age.

it takes three generations to rub away the resilient clay of
her facial praise. teaching daughters and grands to line their
eyes and not read their days she sits shallow as pancake and
considers their ways. when a great-granddaughter stumbles her
way and breaks the bottle of her vanity in the breadth of her
play, she cleans up the glass and she hears herself say *they will
never. know what we look like.*[14]

we need to talk about what we are going to read next. her granddaughter was looking at someone else's granddaughter through the window of the computer and smiling about books. who would have thought of this. who would have thought to think of this. whoever would have dared to mention thinking of the thought of this would have been laughed across the river. her daughter, the giver of computers and other smaller windows, tiny tin cans for keeping in so-called touch, was too much. and did they know what touching was. and were they not themselves what touching does, she wondered. at the real window she could see bernadette's light still on and wonder whether she had fallen asleep in the middle of a romance novel or was awake and breathless now. her own thigh tingling made her think it was the second one. she smiled and wondered would her granddaughter trust her own legs to tell her short-range secrets, to get her to long-distance longings. would she accrue the fondness of absence or would she just text. *girl u up?*[15]

they knew her by her lists. more checkable boxes than hearts.
names, places, and the word *paper* written on paper as in
papers to write and paperwork due, not edges from her paper-
cut hands or anything like that. they knew her by her crosses,
salvation straight lines through the tasks she devastated with
her presence and addiction. sometimes she would almost
pulverize her day, but usually something remained undone.
something stayed unraveling. her spirit saved her from the
death of finishing.[16]

dash of salt in the porridge. (that's good.) calf tension in her high heels. (still got it.) gravel road in her voice come morning. (uh huh.) and the thorns in her rose garden pockets. (oh yes.) minuscule hole in her bucket. (intact.) and a sweetness saved just for the doctor. (mmhmm.) graveyard in the small of her back. (i said.) and african hair in her locket. sugar left in her bowl. (right on.) and milk in her complective coffee. heat where she leaves her behind. (tell the truth.) and sweat where they think she ought to be. salt on the road of her face. (i hear you.) and tautness for tightrope walking. stones in the soles of her shocks. (stay here.) and barbed wire encircling bounty. spout where the day hits bottom. (all right.) and a soft razor under her tongue. stretched out by what she has done. (don't do it.) and tightened by to whom she has done. (well.) cane cutting angles on her legs. (rise sometime.) glands getting active and swole. (now hush.) sun on the day that she borrowed. (write it down.) mineral ground to the ground. rumors made out of her walking. (run on.) rocks in the rocking she feels. (cast not.) sharpness that cuts off her talking. diamond window all open in the back. (come with it.) and a heartbeat for the naked ear. (lub dub.) dirt that disappears. (down and deep.) and sky that waits for rockets. (we have lift.) molasses could melt through her pores. lovers could retrain her breasts. (tsk tsk tsk.) summer for love she can find. (hey celestial.) monsoon for the moment she blessed. (child alive.) ocean for the life that she stole. (amen.)[17]

at last the bruised banister that broke her fall becomes table
leg for the gentrifiers. at last the tin she kept the escape money
in becomes kitchen cred for the kitsch. in the final tally all the
pictures she kept are collage scraps for someone. in the end her
dresses scatter to goodwill. when she is long gone from here,
new neighbors salvage the bathrooms for copper. they take
the handles off the doors that knew how to slam but not how
to save. they will praise the fine patina of the floors she paced.
they will stain the glass of the windows where she pressed her
face and saw she could breathe she could breathe.[18]

The Witnesses the Wayward the Waiting

spill (v)
BRITISH
(in the context of ball games) drop (the ball).

o. eshu wa o. olokun wa o. obatala o. wa o. orisha wa o.
orunmilla wa o. o. wa o. osain wa o. ochosi wa o. obara otura wa
o. osun wa o. wa o. oshun wa wa o. oya wa o. ogun wa o. sango
wa o. wa o. olodumare wa. olodumare waaaa. o. o. o.[1]

the decision was in her legs. how they unlocked at the knee, how they tried to kick tomorrow. how they stretched out of the structure of standing into fly. if she let go they could spell something that anyone could recognize, someone could paint characters if they were watching for the message. but no one is.

no one is watching for the message she can spell with her legs when she lets god through. no one is watching for the message and debating whether it is true. everyone. me and you. we too busy making the mess she gotta leap over.[2]

say it like you love me. say it like that gloss is not the sweat i get working for free for you to feel me unfree me. say it like you know not who i am not, not the dark center of earth your own heart. say it like we are new, factory branded, not as old as hills. say it breathless like helium. so light only white people could have invented us. say it like you miss me like you need me like all this not being around is a knock-kneed mating dance you are dancing just for me. say it like that matters like we are matter like we are not the energy that melts the bars off each other. say it like the drug, not the chisel. say it like we are not stone, we are not solid, we are not staying here. say it baby like this the first time and we are not the hard rock dreams of slaves.[3]

i be that walk a piece of the way home wayward woman. she says.
*i be the butter that makes you love your bread. the part-time lover
that shakes your bed. the sofa woman who chose the street instead.
you don't know me.* she rubs her eyes and tilts her head. *do
you? i am nobody's girl who grows up quick. i am lightning rod and
divining stick, i am the miner's canary and i am sick of the blackness
in your lungs. at the risk of being hung i be that squawking morning
when the rent is due, i be that daughter in the inappropriate shoes.
i be the ankle anchored to the slide in the blues. i be forever. i beat
the weather vane out of vanity cases the who done what out of police
car chases the rhythm out of the musical paces of the hearts on the
hospital hall. i be all. up against satan's wall. evidence of the fall.
pounding sound of the ground when you see me around, try not to
feel lost. feel found.*[4]

he was a crossroads man and everybody knew it. and though
he came home every night he didn't sleep. he could stand in the
middle of the street and know when you would pass before you
even knew you were going to have to go down to the store that
day to get something you were soul sure you already had. he
could even see the horses back then and know that eventually
there would be cars. he felt the orthodontistry of railroad tracks
getting laid in his own smile and he just didn't tell you anything
because you would think he was crazy knowing what only the
ground could know after the ground itself had consulted a root.
he beckoned us with his hands and let us know when to cross
and uncross and when to turn around and go home. he saved
many a marriage that didn't deserve to be saved that way and
gained trust even though we knew he would never be like us,
knew he condescended to associate with those of us who only
knew how to look two ways and then arrogantly called them
"both" as if all there was was up and down the street not the
infinite infinite through.

he wore suspenders and a hat that never quite fell off his head.
he was a thoroughfare man and maybe a bit too much but never
wrong. we thought every town had one until he died and no one
replaced him. he was the only one buried with shoes on when
he laid down his swivel head. guess we'll see him at that other
crossroads, hope he tells us where to go. we are not exactly
catholic but when our spirits can't decide we cross uncross
recross ourselves, longing for what he knows.[5]

that's how she played. like the notes were being stolen from her and would never come back. like each tendon in her hands would miss those sounds when she woke up sore from jook. no one knew where she went to sleep it off all day, but you could hear from anywhere around the swamp her nightmarish call. her beautiful tormented *come on y'all*. in a button-down shirt and long black skirt. she was not who she wanted to be. she was not what you would call free. she was sharecrop to the minor c, she played the edge of things. piano ledge of things. she rarely used the bench. and when the stench of lust and corn liquor was gone there was still the song and the mud and the glut sucked it up till she stopped.[6]

they don't say anything. they don't read lips. they focus on your thighs, keep their hands on their hips. they see right through you. they don't look twice. they use inherited calculations of what's wrong and what's right. they don't paint curves. they just draw lines. they don't trust ribcages. they straighten their spines. fear of the future is all on their faces. curbing your lust is first on their minds.

but they themselves are quare are queer as flowering pines. ancient in their must with the crust of the thousands of times they have opened themselves to flowers, they have penetrated dirt, they have done acrobatics for hours and pretended not to be hurt. they have chased love and cut it right out of their ancient hearts. they have washed and scrubbed and rubbed and teased their ever-complicated parts. they wake up early in the morning and string out curses for the sun.

they mobilize against the heat because they know how deep the heat how sweet the weak how completely the heat

has won.[7]

the skin. it was mostly the gold in the skin they looked for, tracking their wealth defining their health and unclaiming their kin. it was the skin that nearly did them in, their lust to keep (and easily bruise) that yellow reflection of once being used for house servant status obliquely renewed it was the shade that they were tracking for. it was the house maid trade they slackened for and lost the brightness of their eyes and grew a tightness in their thighs that babies crashed against and died dreaming of brown.

they ruled their part of town. though there were less and less to share it with. and throwback children sent and hid with others further north who'd followed lovers, music, or the crazy drum. they held to the story of white columns where they'd come from. they never let you see them sweat or let their variable hair get wet. it was less simple to identify them by the birthmarks and the dimples they interchanged. you only knew their brighter-than-paper-bag range. and kept on walking.

but in the talking we heard of magic uncles and goblin songs and of wrongs and of people turned into dogs and circles with the devil on Saturday nights. which was our way of saying those people just ain't right. they marry their brains out for staying light.[8]

the slate has been through something. whiteness leaves its residue. chalk outlines precede police. the scream of what it means to read right here right now. it is hard blackness children learn to write their names on. the brittle and portable future. shoeless schooldays for bootstrap tannery. hide the welts from welling up with pride. hide the note your parents cannot sign. hide the dust that's ashing up your knees. hide the truest meaning of your time. hide the precious chalk behind your ear. soft between the dreaming of your hair. fill the slate, then wipe and fill again. learn. learn not to write your name in vain.[9]

try to silence the loud. the overly proud. the preacher. the
shroud. the sprung and the plowed. try to leaven the low so
the children can grow but the neighbors won't know, unbossed
but still bowed. try to open the hope with braids and with
rope and with water and soap try to truss out the truth. try to
piecemeal the peace stitch together some sleep and relax for the
reap for the road for the real stuff. try to sap out the stay and
partition the play it is better that way someone whispered once.
try to grow out the grout, groan when you should shout, you
know what it's about, you know you know you know you know
you know you know but you don't hear me though.[10]

this is why the pastor was the past and all the gifts evaporated. this is why the grocer was disgusted with the poison he doled out. this is why the sweeper was the sweetest and the principal was swept away. this is why the teacher touched the chalk like it was clay. this is why the thankless banker bought the same house anyway. and this is why your job is the rip-off version of your day. because you said so.[11]

How We Know

_____

spill (n)
a thin strip of wood or paper used for lighting a fire,
candle, pipe, etc.

once the sky was low. you could taste stars singeing your hair you if you walked around unthinking. once black holes were a literal liability for the living absentminded. once the ancestor stars were not just nightlights to wish upon. they were warnings saying mind your direction. you might get burnt.[1]

lightning doesn't like a lie. she will strike it out of your mouth. she will sear your tongue with knowing what your nonsense attempt was about. she will force you forever to taste all the slop of your slop-seeking snout. so those who tell tales and excuses and mumble when they should shout are responsible for the electric storms you see lighting up the south.[2]

it's a stork story. a southern processed pork story. a secret
Charleston slave port story. the way they tell it is a lot less gory
than birth. it is a story only incidentally of earth and not at all
a story of dirt, the way they tell it. instead of being a story of
soil of blood and oil and bubble and boil, it is a story of flying in
a clean white pouch looped around a bird with a postal job and
good benefits.

what i mean is there is an original sin. or almost original if we
could find a place to begin, trust, they would put it there. and
the way we get human is as vile as swine slaughtered while
walking the assembly line. it is slaveship womb work to make
sure every time humans be what they be. the reproduction of
the unfree orphan children of the sea with time to look but
not to breathe. we weave a web of lies and whitewash it and
give to the birds. the second purpose of the word. the drunk
contingency of capital slurred. have you not heard?

we are not born. we are made. (that's how we get played.)[3]

for eve

you will find her buried in coral and not know. you will find
her in the hardest ground. the rock side can't grow nothing
ground of healing. you will wonder if every hard place is her
bone. you will misunderstand geological time and her strength.
half-life her haunting. you will know her when you see her and
not believe. you will prefer to continue to act as if your world
is solid.[4]

i am before that. i am not born this morning when you
wake up in fear and look frantic for breakfast to belittle, for
something to burn and consume. i am before that. present like
dew and like steam and like dreams without request. i am not
assembled on demand when you suddenly don't know what to
say. i am before that. i am structure of bone. i am contour of
clay. i am paradigm of play. i do not arrive. i stay. i am before
that. i am not invented at the moment in the agenda when the
scapegoat schedule starts. i am before that. i am the drumbeat
that dramatizes the heart. i am the whole point. i am your
favorite part. i am not artifice. i am art.

before black is bad and broken i am more. i am not coin or
token. i am the deepest spell spoken. and you are shook. i am
the energy of birth that you took. i am every blackened letter
pressing on the book. and before that.

before god bless the child that's got her own. i am the moan.
i am the touchstone. i am the divining phone home. i am the
handout that stands out the clarion that shouts we are an
ecosystem.

when slavery is crawling i am grown. i am fierce. i am known. i
am continents wide. the seed is long since sown. i have flown.
when blood becomes brown i am the shaved head crown. deeper
than down i am core. and before. i am more. i am the manna
that neutralizes stores. i am the presence remembered on every
shore. i am the moon in my pull. i am that full.

when domination wants a name i am old. before my sweat is
sold i am gold. i am a circular story retold. i am fire i am root.
i am cavernous ravenous proof. so fly that i precede the lie. so
bright born the same day as the sky.

so just try.[5]

there was a cauldron. that was real. a dark space. a round space. a womblike place for mysteries. there was steam and combination. that was real. and yes. the cauldron may have even been in a cave. a dark space. an echo space. an inner mountain space of home. there was heat at least. and resonance. that's for sure. and outside the cave it was probably night. probably stars out. probably round sound animals awake and active. i would guess that. but probably the truth was simmering all the next day like it do sometimes. and probably that dark combining night, that cave of a temple, that well-used blackened pot was in Africa or your deepest heart. i will give you that.

but that was not where the evil was. that was not it at all. and you know your slander (eye of gander). the evil was that moment when that ladle long and stirring, made to mix and not to menace. made for tasting and basting and trust became a knife for a knight with an ungrounded lust for light, litter, laziness, and leaving.[6]

as if no one lives here. as if the world your shaking creates has no populated underside. as if the lies you tell yourself don't run and hide right in our faces. as if we just emerged this moment when you got in eyeshot. i ought to. shoot you. so you know. that this part hurts.[7]

it's the shoulders in the zoot suit. it's the angry angle. it's the parody. it's the geometry of masculinity revealed without its patent under the slick shellack of hair. it's the not caring that makes them dangerous. makes them dancers even when they walk. makes them seem like they are shouting every time they talk. makes them mean unkillable never hungry and interchangeable. or is it the skin?

the sin of being visible at all pressed up against the night like that.[8]

Picture the house. The house is spilling. There are hands out the window but the doors have barricades. Picture the hands. The hands are crucial. The hands are eloquent they are spelling back their hair. Picture the hair. The hair is heaping. The hair is helping. The hair will overtake. Picture the help. The help are horrified. Their children are learning to dismantle the state.[9]

what is this waking panic call. the gall of morning asking us to rise just to sit back down. we built this town so we could ignore it. we accumulated stuff so we could store it. someone birthed this body and we wore it

down with waste.

add stress to taste maybe a pinch or a peck maybe the rotation of your neck disappearing. nosy neighbors hearing the creak of your bones. maybe it's the phones that made us feel we could do life from a chair and avoid the people of town and their stares and circumvent the sun and its glare while the planet stays in love. and god stays way above looking down sometimes

only to spit.[10]

she eats tape. she swirls it on her fingers tangles it on her tongue she wants to lick the printed sounds off like flavor. the savior. she wants to know what you said.

or is it that all that has been said strangles and eats her instead. crocodile patient lodging her beneath the rock of history the slime the swamp to swallow some lost limb later.

what is our nutritional value in the jaws of history? may we be more than a snack. may we be less than a balanced breakfast. may we each be pebble chokestone gag reflex to digestive destiny regurgitate the rules and start again.[11]

to let the light in. her eyes grow to pools of black spill the edge of her face seek the sun in a solar system that seems to have lost one. and not only that. her womb ticking open inching contract with the universe that she would be the valve the safety if the species were to fail and poison out its own access to sun. she would be the one to restart the universe loving itself black and huge and invisible only to whoever cannot perceive love.[12]

once there were reasons. there were reasons why we walked. reasons why we touched each other and talked. once we could taste the seasons in the air and we repeated them to each other. we were present with each other once. at least the old ones like to believe that. once we were alive together not inside some story about everything we are afraid of as inevitable. the only thing that can happen being hurt. once upon a time we were making the story not taking it in like corn syrup and blood. once we came to each other with integrity and interest not salt and pepper spray. we loved our mouths. once we thought it was valuable to breathe. to share air to wonder where the other of us might end up one day. once we knew that we did not know and we cherished it. the wondering. now we are policing wandering. we perceive no one to be where they belong. once we just longed for understanding and underlined it with a song, now our stomachs are lined with lead. now our children are better off dead than being what we think of them.[13]

i saw him in the corner of a photograph, his accidental fingertip interrupting the pose. maybe he was supposed to be taking the picture or taking the camera away from our souls. i saw him on a postcard on a caption about a landscape. open space all named after him absence hailed. the card didn't have enough postage to get to where it was going but the postmarks on the back say it bounced around the world. i saw him underwater when i was flying on a plane and the silver in the clouds said you will never see him again. but i saw him yesterday on lifetime tv. the perfect man who will save us and set us all free.[14]

The Way

---

verb: **spill**; 3rd person present: **spills**; past tense: **spilt**; past participle: **spilt**; past tense: **spilled**; past participle: **spilled**; gerund or present participle: **spilling**

there was always the one. that walked the dirt path crooked infringing on the grass. that cleared the forest in some adinkra design that for sure could only be seen from heaven. that wore out the outside of one shoe and the inside of the other from their everyday crooked tendencies. the one that danced, planted, plotted, and eventually drove as if he was falling down, as if her ear loved the ground, as if he was suspended from above by a lazy god she loved enough to keep believing in.

there was one. every village, every small town, eventually every zip code had one. and needed that one so they could measure their straightness, ninety-degree their angles, perpendicular their walks. you know, relief. but then something happened and the sideways dancers, dirt path deviators, asymptote tracers started to lean towards each other more and more and they found each other on corners stunned and grateful to have people who could look into their diagonal eyes, their own people with no desire to adjust their half-cocked hats. they found each other and they reshaped the streets together with their feet tending to tiltsphere.

and the townships who had lost their tilters questioned their own straightness, shaped themselves to questions, curved in other ways. they didn't think to wish that their crooked fools had stayed, they just looked up to the sky and asked and listened to the ground and didn't realize that their angles grew acutely towards the sound of walking sideways and they found themselves leaving town down the same routes that had erstwhile always led them home. they roamed out of earshot of the talking drums and bells that had forever held them well and they found music that made them doubt and made them jump and tilt and shout. they found each other.

and then the tilting magic spread like a lightness in the head, an orientation towards the dead while we're still living. and our streets became forgiving and our buildings became round and we gave up straightness and guess what? nothing was missing.[1]

she started with jars. stashed when no one was thinking about
canning. when the sun was still in love and loath to leave us
and when sun finally did leave light winked back through the
bellies of bugs. it was a heat she did not want to live without
kissing her heartbeat hands. it was sweet childish lantern-
making at first. expected. the intensity of her swoon sway
dance with the grass and the insects was neglected by teenagers
and adults who had other forms of love to attend to without
seeming like it. in a way she was more honest than any of us.
more faithful than most. and while the crushes of our summers
flickered on and off at twilight she was already insisting beyond
the season. she was unnatural really. unsuited for a world that
dressed itself in lies, that allowed bodies and promises to shed
themselves and die. she was not like that. but then on the other
hand what is more natural than letting summer into your skin.
and wouldn't you keep it if you could? my sci-fi reading cousin
says she had a special kind of melanin. i say she remembered
something the rest of us forgot. my son says she's the first mad
scientist he ever heard about.

but this was all after the fact. all we know is we rarely saw her
in winter and when we did she wasn't dressed for it. and her red
sundress always fit and her skin always stayed so smooth. and
when her pretty man whom no one knew and some said was
too pretty to be a man at all left her towards the beginning of
the fall that year a thunderbolt struck one time and split all the
trees leading out of town.[2]

her fingerprints rewritten rivers of coconut oil and shea.
strands the geological memories punctuating the groove and
hands god herself who moves and moves and moves. some
would say she is slick. some would say she is thick. most
would not say she is soaked in the universe. most would not
compare the tiny ridges on her fingertips to the oldest forms
of script. most would not connect the floorboards of her porch
to the roots that they remember when she sits. most would
not observe her face looking for patterns that are visible from
space. her clients keep their backs to her. they have no eyes
for what she sees. and the sea? well. they forget the ocean.
themselves. but the desert. they remember enough to long for
moisture. and to trust.

her eyelids know streambeds are pathways. know water from
sky. know there is a spiritual reason why your scalp is dry. know
cornrows from ricefields know laurels from crowns know most
hieroglyphics are nouns. but her fingers speak present tense
like weather and how. and her works of art feel pain but know
better than to howl. they don't understand the tapestry on
their shoulders is a towel. but they know enough to sit up tall.
they sure know not to scream. and when she's finished they
recognize themselves as a forgotten black dream.

even air becomes a ribbon even silence has a scent even
laughter gets braided even split ends repent. and the pattern in
her breathing settles sweetly on their pores and the unlocked
locks of tangle get unnetted from the shore. and all the elders
know to say is: she has been here before.

it looks like whirlwind. it feels like your head is shrinking. it
smells like heaven. it tastes like salt. it sounds slightly like a
waterfall. it goes like this:

massage out monday massage in more massage through
mandate awaken the core. part practice from patience part

CONTINUED

what they say from what you know part partness from
wholeness part being from show. braid fear over faith under
throughline walking home. twist and repeat. braid faith over
fear underneath speech. add in one perfect day with delicious
food and plenty of sleep. coil coolness up and through sheen
spray with sunbaked heat. and repeat and repeat and repeat
and repeat. some only come out of the sense that they should
sit down. but she makes sure they stand up. crowned.[3]

(or skateboard sorcerer sacrifice)

believe they can fly. are willing to fall. trust the resilience of
their sweet brown flesh more than they fear to break their
only white bones. they are the gladiators unhelmeted refusing
the straightness of railings or streets. they are the asphalt
community of black enough to dance stretch flex and compete.
sidebody wings they are messengers. bold black fleet. they will
sacrifice elbows knees brains and backsides. there is no limit to
the gravel they will eat. black bodies breakable brave and awake
demanding justice from the ground with that beat.[4]

it was the taste in her mouth as the paper flew from windows, as the sneakers snuck away as the plate glass ate its meaning. it was the strange blue light of irrelevant police. as if aliens had landed and retail had run to meet them. it was night by the time the people remembered to be wild. or maybe they thought the moon a more militant god than sun. or maybe like everything else rebellion waited until the chores were done. or maybe they finally remembered what darkness was and broke the streetlights.

latent harriet tubman night vision became the new liberation ink. and quiet bass in songs of freedom caused the revolutionaries to think this chaos was not new but destined and her mouth tasted like zinc. it was her own blood.[5]

they drip with it. their resistant hip bones etch it deep into brick walls. their unschooled mouths spill it all over the sidewalk. their rubber shoe prints burn stamps with every shuffled step. they cannot be ignored. they hold and drop the prop, the show that blows the minds of their own kind, the dance of no first or second chance. the molten rage. they act their age. they the players you the stage. they are the ink, the world's the page. take note take heed engage the game. release your breath. unlearn your shame. resume your size. stand down. stand down and recognize. the future writing its name.[6]

someone wrapped it in newspaper and put it in the closet. someone hid it for safekeeping in a cake. someone shredded it into tiny unstealable pieces. someone buried it surreptitiously in a lake. someone ate it because digesting it was better. someone flushed it because they thought they heard the cops. someone gave it to a child who dropped it somewhere. someone pawned it at the worst point in a breakup (then they stacked it in the back room of the shop). someone checked it in a bag that never got there. someone set it on the roof and drove away. and they all probably think that they still have it. they don't. (you have to use it every day.)[7]

ACKNOWLEDGMENTS

How

Because of my mothers. Because of my fathers. Because of my teachers. Because of my witnesses. Because of my sisters. Because of my brothers. Because of all my relations. Because of my community. Because of my collaborators. Because of our ancestors. Because of the sweet purveyors of our unpromised future. Because of my champion. You know who you are. Multitudes. Thank you.

I would especially like to thank my parents, Pauline McKenzie and Clyde Gumbs; my mentor, Cheryll Greene; and my partner, Julia Roxanne Wallace/Sangodare, for their love and support.

"daughters have their own agendas" was inspired by Amaya Claire Jacques, daughter of the artist Soraya Jean-Louis McElroy and founder of the Black Magnolias reading group.

"is a question we cannot politely ask" was inspired by the brave poetry and mothering of Joy KMT.

Everyone at Duke University Press and especially Ken Wissoker, Jade Brooks, Nicole Campbell, Jessica Ryan, and the anonymous readers blessed me with their enthusiasm, attention, and specificity.

Short excerpts of *Spill* were published as:

- "sticks and bricks might break our bones, but words will most certainly kill us," *Wild Flor y Canto*, Seeds of Resistance zine (2014).

- "black studies and all its children" and "menaced by everything and nothing in particular," *Eleven Eleven*, no. 17 (Summer 2014).

- "why be content with the lightning bug when you can have the lightning," *As Us* (October 2014).

- "black studies and all its children," in *Best American Experimental Fiction 2015*, edited by Douglas Kearney (Middletown, CT: Wesleyan University Press, 2016).

- "weave of motives" in "Experiments in Joy," special issue of *Obsidian: Literature and Arts in the African Diaspora* (Spring 2016).

NOTES

All notes in the text refer to Hortense Spillers, *Black, White, and in Color: Essays on American Literature and Culture* (Chicago: University of Chicago Press, 2003). The epigraph to "Appendix: A Note" is from "Whatcha Gonna Do?: Revisiting 'Mama's Baby, Papa's Maybe: An American Grammar Book': A Conversation with Hortense Spillers, Saidiya Hartman, Farah Jasmine Griffin, Shelley Eversley, and Jennifer L. Morgan," *Women's Studies Quarterly* 35, nos. 1/2 (Spring–Summer 2007): 299–309.

/ / /

HOW SHE KNEW

1 **unalterable badness** "A Hateful Passion, a Lost Love," 95.
2 **immersed in the material** "A Hateful Passion, a Lost Love," 100.
3 **new world callaloo, return over and over again** Introduction, 2.
4 **attack in its historic signature** Preface, xvii.
5 **on the prowl for new religions** "Formalism Comes to Harlem," 85.
6 **It's something one makes against the force of his or her intuition** "Formalism Comes to Harlem," 82.
7 **altered human tissue** "Mama's Baby, Papa's Maybe," 207.

8 **a symptom of the inevitable** "Formalism Comes to Harlem," 87; **analogously terrible weight** "Mama's Baby, Papa's Maybe," 203.

9 **a new dimension of being** "A Hateful Passion, a Lost Love," 93.

10 **new female being** "A Hateful Passion, a Lost Love," 93.

11 **quirkiness of conception** Introduction, 2.

12 **begins at the "beginning" which is really a rupture** "Mama's Baby, Papa's Maybe," 209.

13 **new female being (2.0)** "A Hateful Passion, a Lost Love," 93.

HOW SHE SPELLED IT

1 **vision-in-dream-brought-on-by-other-power** "Ellison's 'Usable Past,'" 72.

2 **hieroglyphics of the flesh** "Mama's Baby, Papa's Maybe," 207.

3 **necessary critical fable** "A Hateful Passion, a Lost Love," 481n3.

4 **Sticks and bricks *might* break our bones, but words will most certainly *kill* us**. "Mama's Baby, Papa's Maybe," 207 (emphasis in the original).

5 **a past too much to evoke all at once** Introduction, 33.

6 **put the question on the table** Introduction, 47.

7 **meanings of womanhood which statements of public policy are rhetorically bound to repress** "A Hateful Passion, a Lost Love," 111.

8 **The question splinters down to the central rib** Introduction, 40.

9 **profound changes in aesthetic surface** "Ellison's 'Usable Past,'" 65.

10 **this fragmented legacy—these shards of broken desire** Introduction, 40.

11 **symbol smasher** "A Hateful Passion, a Lost Love," 93.

12 **Not everybody knows my name** "Mama's Baby, Papa's Maybe," 203.

HOW SHE LEFT

1 **It tells far less than it shows** "Ellison's 'Usable Past,'" 68.

2 **whatever arises freely, spontaneously in the human being's**

address to his or her environment "Formalism Comes to Harlem," 82.

3 **"Slave" is perceived as the essence of stillness** "Mama's Baby, Papa's Maybe," 224.

4 **That is one kind of strategic decision, there are others** "A Hateful Passion, a Lost Love," 109.

5 **one never gets very far without her mother** Preface, xviii.

6 **in this case we embrace untruth gladly** "Formalism Comes to Harlem," 88.

7 **a calculus of motives that we call modernity** Introduction, 42.

8 **what oracular fever** "A Hateful Passion, a Lost Love," 112.

9 **await whatever marvels of my own inventiveness** "Mama's Baby, Papa's Maybe," 203.

10 **a discourse ordained by history** "A Hateful Passion, a Lost Love," 98.

11 **the violence, forgetfulness, and contradictions which surround the surrogate name** "Formalism Comes to Harlem," 92.

HOW SHE SURVIVED UNTIL THEN

1 **the ambiguities of mercy** "A Hateful Passion, a Lost Love," 113.

2 **riddled by tribalistic implications** "Formalism Comes to Harlem," 85.

3 **Language does speak** "Ellison's 'Usable Past,'" 66.

4 **This is the domain of invisibility** "Ellison's 'Usable Past,'" 71.

5 **loyal to the idiom of comic sabotage** "Formalism Comes to Harlem," 82.

6 **Language is an act of concealment** "Ellison's 'Usable Past,'" 66.

7 **oxygen supply of the social upside down** Introduction, 20.

8 **If I were not here I would have to be invented** "Mama's Baby, Papa's Maybe," 203.

9 **brewing under the bed** "Formalism Comes to Harlem," 92 (citing a conversation with Toni Cade Bambara).

10 **But the fiction of differences is something else again** Introduction, 21.

11 **the perfect bind situation** Introduction, 12.

WHERE SHE ENDED UP

THE WAY

BIBLIOGRAPHY
Indirect References and Suggested Reading

Bambara, Toni Cade, ed. *The Black Woman*. New York: Signet, 1970.

———. *The Salt Eaters*. New York: Random House, 1980.

———. *Those Bones Are Not My Child*. New York: Doubleday, 2009.

Bandele, Asha. *Daughter*. New York: Scribner, 2005.

———. *Something Like Beautiful: One Single Mother's Story*. New York: Harper, 2009.

Brand, Dionne. *At the Full and Change of the Moon*. Toronto: Grove, 1999.

Brooks, Gwendolyn. *The Bean Eaters*. Chicago: Third World, 1960.

———. *Maud Martha*. Chicago: Third World, 1953.

Brown, Ruth Nicole. *Hear Our Truths: The Creative Potential of Black Girlhood*. Urbana: University of Illinois Press, 2013.

Butler, Octavia. *Parable of the Sower*. New York: Warner, 1993.

Chancy, Myriam. *The Scorpion's Claw*. Leeds, UK: Peepal Tree, 2005.

Cox, Aimee Meredith. *Shapeshifters: Black Girls and the Choreography of Citizenship*. Durham, NC: Duke University Press, 2015.

Davis, Thulani. *1959*. New York: Grove, 1992.

De Veaux, Alexis. *Blue Heat*. New York: Diva Publishing, 1985.

———. *Yabo*. Silver Spring, MD: Redbone, 2014.

Finney, Nikky. *Rice*. Toronto: Sistervision, 1995.

———. *The World Is Round*. Atlanta: InnerLight Books, 2003.

Flack, Roberta. *The First Take*. LP. Atlantic Records, 1969.

Frazier, Demita, Barbara Smith, and Beverly Smith. *The Combahee River Collective Statement*. 1977; reprint, Latham, NY: Kitchen Table, 1986.

Golden, Marita. *The Edge of Heaven*. New York: Ballantine, 1998.

Hurston, Zora Neale. *Spunk*. New York: Marlowe, 1997.

———. *Their Eyes Were Watching God*. New York: J. B. Lippincott, 1937.

Jones, Tayari. *Leaving Atlanta*. New York: Warner, 2002.

———. *Silver Sparrow*. Chapel Hill, NC: Algonquin, 2011.

———. *The Untelling*. New York: Warner, 2005.

Jordan, June. *Civil Wars*. Boston: Beacon, 1981.

———. "The Difficult Miracle of Black Poetry in America or Something Like a Sonnet for Phillis Wheatley." *On Call*. Boston: Beacon, 1985.

———. *On Call*. Boston: Beacon, 1985.

———. *Passion*. Boston: Beacon, 1980.

———. "Poem about My Rights." *Passion*. Boston: Beacon, 1980.

Lorde, Audre. *The First Cities*. Broadside, 1968.

———. "Now That I Am Forever with Child." *The First Cities*. Broadside, 1968.

Mathis, Ayana. *The Twelve Tribes of Hattie*. New York: Vintage, 2012.

Mootoo, Shani. *Cereus Blooms at Night*. Toronto: Grove, 2009.

Moraga, Cherie. *A Xicana Codex of Changing Consciousness*. Durham, NC: Duke University Press, 2011.

Morrison, Toni. *Beloved*. New York: Random House, 1987.

———. *Home*. New York: Random House, 2012.

———. *Song of Solomon*. New York: Random House, 1977.

———. *Sula*. New York: Random House, 1973.

Naylor, Gloria. *Linden Hills*. New York: Penguin, 1986.

———. *Mama Day*. New York: Penguin, 1988.

Phillip, Marlene Nourbese. *Looking for Livingstone: An Odyssey of Silence*. Stanford, ON: Mercury, 1991.

———. *She Tries Her Tongue Her Silence Softly Breaks*. Havana: Casa de Las Americas, 1988.

———. *Zong*. Middletown, CT: Wesleyan University Press, 2008.

Phillips, Rasheedah. *Recurrence Plot: And Other Time Travel Tales*. Philadelphia: Afro-Futurist Affair, 2014.

Shange, Ntozake. *Betsey Brown*. New York: St. Martin's, 1985.

———. *for colored girls who have considered suicide/when the rainbow is enuf*. New York: St. Martin's, 1975.

———. "With No Immediate Cause." *Nappy Edges*. New York: St. Martin's, 1978.

Simone, Nina. *Nina Simone at Town Hall*. LP. Colpix Records, 1959.

Smith, Barbara, ed. *Home Girls: A Black Feminist Anthology*. Latham, NY: Kitchen Table, 1983.

Smith, Barbara, Akasha Gloria Hull, and Patricia Bell-Scott, eds. *All the Women Are White, All the Blacks Are Men, but Some of Us Are Brave*. New York: Feminist Press, 1982.

Thomas, Sheree. *Dark Matter: A Century of Science Fiction from the African Diaspora*. New York: Warner Aspect, 2000.

Trethewey, Natasha. *Bellocq's Ophelia*. Minneapolis: Graywolf, 2002.

———. *Domestic Work*. Minneapolis: Graywolf, 2000.

———. *Native Guard*. New York: Mariner, 2007.

Walker, Alice. *The Color Purple*. New York: Harcourt, 1982.

———. *In Love and Trouble*. New York: Harcourt, 1967.

———. *Meridian*. New York: Harcourt, 1976.

———. *The Third Life of Grange Copeland*. New York: Harcourt, 1970.

Wheatley, Phillis. *Poems on Various Subjects*. London, 1773.

Williams, Angel Kyodo. *Being Black: Zen and the Art of Living with Fearlessness*. New York: Penguin, 2002.

Youngblood, Shay. *The Big Mama Stories*. Ann Arbor, MI: Firebrand, 1989.